English Fluency For Asian Speakers

Accent reduction for Chinese, Japanese, and Korean

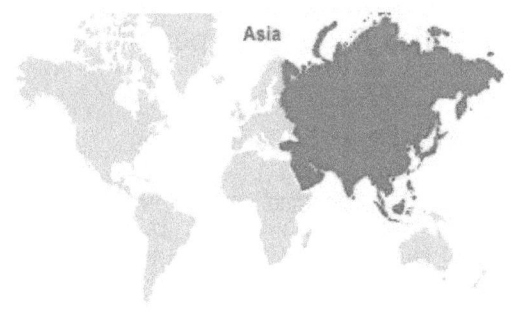

Asia

Whitney Nelson

Contents

Conclusion

7 Successful Steps to Accent Reduction for Asian Students

Chapter 1: Stage Fright Speaks in Every Language, but . . .

Fear # 1 – I'm embarrassed by my foreign accent

Even the Dalai Lama can be Misunderstood

Fear #2: What if I can't find the right English words for my topic.

Fear # 3 – Is my English going to be easily Understood?

Fear # 4 – I'm afraid my presentation will be boring because I speak too slowly

Fear # 5 – Will I understand the audience's questions?

Chapter 2: Practice your English Before you're scheduled to Present

No Time Like the Present.

Don't Trust Your Memory to Speak Off the Cuff

Write the Speech Out in English.

Read Your Speech Out Loud

Create a Set of Notes based on your Speech.

Practice Presenting your Speech

Record your Presentation during your Practice Sessions

Reverse Accent Mimicry

Practice. Record, repeat. Review.

Alternate your Practice Material

Listen to Four Areas

Introduction: Speak Like a Native Speaker

There's a wonderful scene in an episode of the television show, the Big Bang Theory, in which Raj, one of the four "nerdy" physicists buys his first iPhone with voice recognition. He insists there's something wrong with it, though.

Every time he attempts to ask Siri, the name of the voice on the phone, she claims she can't understand him.

Can you relate to this scenario? Did you believe that you had nearly overcome your accent and spoke nearly like a native – until you tried talking to Siri?

No doubt, that was a heck of a wake-up call. You aren't alone in your inability to talk to Siri. Many accent reduction trainers reported an immense growth of students following the release of the voice-recognition technology.

Now that you've gotten over the shock, you're probably ready to get on with the rest of your English language education and practice. It clearly appears that voice recognition is the wave of the future.

And this technology is only in its infancy. Alexa, a product from Google, stands by in a cylinder that you can place conveniently on your table – or anywhere for that matter – available to answer any question you may have. This same technology is also slowly taking hold in many new cars.

That's only one small problem you may encounter if your Asian accent makes it difficult for others to understand your English. There may be other telltale signs that your spoken word isn't as clear and "American-like" as you would like them to be.

Have you reached a plateau in your work at school and you're not quite sure why?

Perhaps you've abruptly knocked up against the proverbial glass ceiling in your career?

Because English is your second language, you pause for a few moments to wonder if it isn't your Asian accent – Japanese, Korean or Chinese for instance – that's holding you back.

You watch other Asian students at your school or your colleagues at your place of employment make strides toward advancement and promotion. Quite frankly, you finally admit, you do experience at least a bit of jealousy. You wonder why they get the promotions, the better grades and not you.

Then it dawns on you. They all speak English fluently. They sound so close to a native speaker that you can't help admire them at the same time you're jealous of them.

What is the Secret to Fluency in English?

That leads you to the natural questions:

What makes these fluent speakers different from you?

Does it come down to a natural talent for languages that you don't possess? Or did they do something you failed to do? And, if so, is it too late to learn what it was?

It's natural for these and many more questions to be racing through your mind as you try to analyze if you can still do something – anything – to reach the point of fluency.

The truth of the matter is that *it's never too late to gain fluency in English.* Regardless of how many years you've been studying you too can learn the secrets of those who speak fluent English.

Not only that, you'll be pleasantly surprised to discover that it takes but a few changes in your speech along with some practice to notice the difference. All you need to do is to learn the secrets that every Asian student fluent in English already knows.

Perhaps you've already noticed that those Asian students who speak fluently are, more often than not, perceived to be smarter than those who retain their Asian accent. And, in turn, they're the ones who are being offered the promotions – despite the fact that you might be more qualified and, quite frankly, inherently brighter and more insightful.

This succinct book covers various concepts, ideas, and techniques to help lift you off your English language plateau and take you to the next level of learning. When you follow the tips and tricks and discover a few of the more stubborn obstacles preventing you from reducing your accent, then you'll begin to sound more like a native and your self-confidence will skyrocket. Guaranteed.

5 Keys to Fluent English

Each individual Asian student and professional no doubt took his or her own path to developing their command of the English language. If you were to take a survey, however, you'd no doubt find that they implemented at least of a few – if not all of these five "secrets of fluency":

1. Learn where the hidden "z" sounds are in many English plural words and when to pronounce them.

2. Discover the proper way to enunciate the five English vowels – a, e, i, o, u.

3. Asian students and professionals fluent in English know that one of the keys to fluency is correctly stressing syllables – the smallest part

of any English word. Once you conquer this, you too will be speaking the language with a flair you've never thought possible. In addition to revealing how these techniques of pronunciation can help you get to your next promotion and increase your confidence in school, you'll learn the best way to practice English to get you to fluency quicker and faster.

4. This book explains how the method of "immersion" can increase your fluency. In these pages, you'll learn exactly what immersion is and how, even if you're not surrounded by native speakers, you can experience this powerfully productive process.

5. That's only one of many methods you'll learn. This book will also help you learn how your mirror can be your best friend in reaching fluency and how a method called "reverse mimicry" have already taken many from being self-conscious about their accent to self-confidence about their discussions and presentations.

You'll discover, thanks to the concise presentations in this volume, that you can catapult your level of fluency before you know it. Then it's only a short time after that you'll notice that your colleagues and fellow students will think more highly of you. And that you're the one others are envying because you're the one on the receiving end of the promotions.

Are you ready? It's time to get started!

Chapter 1: The Importance of Speaking English Fluently

You may feel like sounding like a native is an unreachable goal. You may even have your moments of abandoning that goal and settling for the pronunciation you currently use.

Many Asian students of English as a second language feel that way at one time or another. Heck, many native speakers feel the same way. Those with strong regional accents would love nothing better than to reduce or eliminate their accents totally.

Don't start brooding on this. It's natural, of course. You've worked hard to learn English and we all know it's not an easy language to learn. But, when you began your journey, I'm sure you had your personal reasons why you wanted to learn it.

Think back to when you first start learning the language. You probably were enthusiastic, eager to soak up every aspect of English and looking forward to all the doors this language would open for you. If you learned it as quickly as many Asian students and even adults, you knew that speaking like a native would provide you with untold opportunities.

Learning English, no doubt, filled your self-confidence and buoyed you to meet the future full of hope.

Consider the following question and answer it realistic. Has your knowledge of English got you as far as you wanted it to – in either school or your career? If not, then you still have some more planning and studying to do. If you hesitated in answering, then the mere fact that you're reading this book provides you with an answer to that question.

When you first started learning English you knew inherently that it was an important step in your academic or professional career, even if you weren't completely sure what doors or opportunities this valuable language could open for you.

Why not pause for a moment now to recall the reasons why were so adamant to learn this language. Think back for a moment now about what your personal and career goals were when you first started learning. To help encourage you in this process, recall and relive the high hopes you had for learning English. Those reasons are, no doubt, still as valid now as when you first made them.

Now think back to how optimistic you felt. It's time to focus once again on your personal goals and regain the feeling of excitement and eagerness you experienced.

Aside from your own reasons for learning English, linguists have cited their own reasons for recommending Asians learn this language. Some of the most crucial reasons are listed below.

Proper English Brands you as an Educated Person

It's true!

Rightly or wrongly, strangers will hear your fluency in the language and their first impression is one of a highly educated person. That means they will give your views, your opinions more weight. When you speak, many people will listen a little closer, consider your opinions a little longer and give you more credit for being overall a better-educated individual, much more aware of the events around you.

If you need confirmation of this, just take a survey of the real "movers and shakers" of society. These individuals include senior corporate executives, professionals, government officials and more. Surprisingly (or perhaps not so surprisingly), this drive and uniting force of these highly success people cut across all ethnicity lines.

There's no better way to test this concept than to learn to speak English fluently so you can see for yourself the differences in how you're viewed.

You may want to give up or settle for an accent with an excuse here or one there. While you may think, offhand that football players and other athletes, don't necessarily depend on proper English for their success. All they need to do, you may think is to learn how to play the game.

That couldn't be anything farther from the truth. Not only will you be requested to speak occasionally to the press, but every valuable teammate needs to be able to communicate with the others.

As a fluent English speaker, you'll also become a more attractive job candidate.

Your fluency in English tells your potential employee more than that you've just taken the time to learn the language. It brands you as a person who is bright and persistent. Your fluency makes the person who is considering hiring you fairly confident that you'll put that same persistence in working your best as an employee.

Many potential employers will also recognize that's it's no easy feat to learn a second language – and be fluent. It's a subtle way to show your natural intelligence without saying outright, "I'm a smart person."

You Need to Reduce Your Accent when Working in an International Marketplace

Believe it or not, there is probably no type of business that is contained within its national borders in the twenty-first century.

English has been labeled "the language of business." There's a lot of truth in that. Even if you don't travel overseas for your career, there are several ways this language may still be invaluable to your business dealings:

First, speaking English without an Asian accent puts you at the head of the class when it comes to **conducting international business meetings.** If several languages are represented in these meetings – as often are – you may be, at the very least, the first choice of your supervisors to attend international meetings.

Being fluent in English – without an accent – puts you first in line for **customer service and sales positions.** The great thing about this career is that it positions you to make contacts and network with businesses internationally. Not only are these contacts healthy for your personal career, they'll also help you promote and promulgate your business as well.

In a career in this area, being fluent in at least two languages depending on your background and education – with one of them being English – can make you a rising star in your chosen field.

Fluency in English also makes you a perfect candidate for **positions in marketing and communications.**

The firm for which you work may market and sell its products to English-speaking languages. At the very least, you may be the go-to person to translate the marketing and public relations materials to English.

But that's not the only advantage you'll have in these departments over other employees. As part of your learning the English language, you've also learned much about the cultures of those countries where English is spoken. Think about it. You'll possess the insight into how potential customers think and what motivates them to purchase your company's product.

Perhaps thirty years ago, speaking without an accent was less crucial. But, given the pervasiveness of the internet and the corresponding shrinking of national borders and barriers, your desire to reduce or eliminate your accent is a wise move.

Setting your Sights on an Academic Career?

The same arguments hold true. Not only will eliminating your Asian accent help you in so many ways in college, the elimination of your accent may open opportunities at some of the best universities in the world.

It's true! English is, without a doubt, viewed as the language of higher education. Think of the list of schools whose doors will now be open to you. Massachusetts Institute of Technology, Harvard, Yale, Cambridge, Oxford. The list may not be infinite, but it certainly is a dazzling selection. The few universities listed here are only the tip of the iceberg. Get fluent in English and the sky's the limit.

Discussion-Based Courses

Once you do choose the school of your choice, you're speaking English without a hint of an accent will help you in so many courses. For example, there are any number of courses that are discussion-based. Think philosophy here as well as history, sociology or any other humanity-based subject. You'll be better understood and both professors and fellow students alike will give your opinion more weight.

With you speak with a reduced accent, it very well could be you're improving your chances at being a teaching assistant. In this graduate student position, you spend one or two classes a week with undergraduates in discussion sections whose topics are what had been covered in the professor's lectures. These can be very useful to students who need items clarified.

Without that accent, you'll feel much more confident and comfortable helping these students.

There are many reasons to choose to reduce and eliminate your Asian accent. The reasons here are only a few of some of the best. You've already recalled your original reasons why you wanted to learn to speak the language. You're so close to speaking fluency you can feel it.

This is no time to say, "That's it! I give up. This is as far as I'm going!" There's no better time than to dig in and get rid of the accent and speak English like a native.

In the next chapter, we'll discuss one of the best known, most popular and some say most effective methods of not only learning English but reducing and even eliminating your Asian accent.

Chapter 2: Immersion: Is it the Best Way to Reduce your Accent?

As a student of English as a second language, you may have already heard about the technique called immersion. It's a method that some professional linguists and teachers say is not only the most effective method of gaining fluency in a language but the easiest as well.

In fact, up to six-five percent of all linguists believe that immersion is the fastest way to learn a language.

Technically speaking this terms describes – quite well, as a matter of fact – the process by which academic students learn to speak a second language within the classroom setting. From the moment students step into the classroom to the moment the class is over no instruction in any other language is provided.

Depending on your view, this could be considered a sink-or-swim situation. While it's the best way to learn, this method's success depends on the willingness and the desire of the student to learn the language. Specifically, it originally applied to younger, elementary students who are known for soaking up and learning languages quickly and easily.

In this way, the students learn through intuition other ways to speak English. Since no other language is spoken in the classroom, even if a child does ask questions in his native tongue, he is instructed to ask in English. Eventually, the children learn the words and even the structure of the language while they are learning vocabulary.

Mind you now, the students, at first, may not learn grammar and the other finer points of the language through formal lessons at this time. But by listening to a native speaker, who does converse in proper grammar, they have no choice but to emulate the instructors.

As you might guess, there is one disadvantage to immersion through classroom experience. Sure, you'll be learning proper English and correct grammar. But it'll also be the most sterile English you've ever heard.

What does that mean?

It means that while correct, the chances are good that's not the way most Americans speak the language on the streets and in the privacy of their homes. After several years of classroom instruction with this method, you'll certainly be able to walk out of the room with impeccable English, but you may sound stilted and just as sterile as the language you're speaking.

Today, though, the immersion technique has a much farther reaching meaning. It's a term that's used whenever students of English place themselves in situations in which English is the only language they are expected to speak as well as the only language others speak to them.

While immersion has long been considered effective for adult students of the language, for the longest time it has also been the most elusive way for many to study. Unfortunately, for the longest time for adults, the only way to implement the concept of immersion was to live in the country for a minimum of several months. This, obviously wasn't realistic for many people, especially for students.

Thanks to the ever-increasing spread of technology, any English student can immerse themselves just about on command. Not only that, but they can control the length and the depth of their immersion. While the possibilities aren't endless, they are, indeed, varied.

That's fine, you're thinking. But you've already conquered some of the hardest aspects of speaking English. You're only searching for ways and methods to eliminate your accent. What exactly does that have to do with me? You may be surprised to learn the immersion method can also help you speak English like a native speaker, that is, accent-free.

Of course, ask anyone who is knowledgeable in learning languages and they'll agree the best way to learn to reduce your accent is by talking with real native speakers in person. They urge whenever possible you do just that. Immersing yourself in the language means you're placing yourself in a situation in which you have almost no choice but to listen to your accent and work on perfecting your pronunciation of your most troublesome sounds and words.

They are, indeed, confident that immersion is a viable and efficient way to speak like you've been speaking English your entire life. But they also admit that it's possible to reduce your accent and learn how natives approach speaking their language through a form of immersion that utilizes such technology, including the internet as well as television, cable and satellite shows.

Yes, finally television – notoriously maligned as a vast wasteland – has at least one positive use. Students of English as a second language have long been encouraged to watch a variety to help them reduce their accent.

Be an Active Listener

This may sound simple enough, but while you're watching these shows – and any English-language television program will work, you need to be an active and not a passive listener. What is an active listener?

It's a given, at your current level of fluency, that there will be few words you won't know the meaning to. So you won't need to listen intently trying to recall the meaning or even for how the English language is used structurally.

Your mission, then, is to listen with an ear of how these words are pronounced.

The beauty of using this technology is that you're in charge of the material you use to develop your skills. In the past, many students lost enthusiasm for learning a language simply because the material they had to listen to was . . . was, frankly, boring.

So, you're encouraged to choose your favorite shows, topics and any other material that's available to you and spoken in English. There's no doubt that when you're engaged in the story line with characters you've come to like and to whom you can relate, you'll be able to reduce your accent much more quickly.

There is one caveat, though. It's best, at least part of the time, that you watch your favorite shows alone. In this way, you can sit there and repeat any words you may believe you're speaking improperly.

Don't be afraid to sit and watch some of the same episodes over and over again. (Here again is another reason why you want to consider watching the shows alone.). Eventually, you'll be saying the same lines with the characters. This means that you'll become familiar with the way Americans speak their language. Keep repeating the words you feel give you a tough time.

One of the best ways to do this in this day of technology is with the subscriber service Netflix. Yes, believe it or not, this could become one of the best tools at your disposal to help you overcome your accent.

If you've never watched any show on this service, then you may not know that there is a bar at the bottom of your screen that allows you to pause the movie or television shows at any time. Most of us pause to either run into the kitchen for a bite to eat or for a bathroom break. There's no reason why you can't pause the show after you've heard a word you just can't seem to enunciate correctly, though.

Pause the show. Repeat the word several times. Go back to that same word and compare your pronunciation with the characters. Do this several times. As you practice this "rewinding method", you'll soon develop your own personal technique that works best for you.

Even if you don't subscribe to Netflix, you have the opportunity with several of the sites on the internet, most notably youtube.com. If you believe that the only things you can find on this site are recordings of funny cats and talking dogs, you're wrong. (And come to think of it, why not repeat what a talking dog is saying as long as he doesn't have any noticeable accent of his own.)

There are plenty of solid English-speaking videos on a variety of topics from online marketing to the fall of Rome and UFO's. Got a favorite topic? Search for it on YouTube and take a listen. Again, you're listening with an intent of reducing your accent. So keep in mind you're an active listener through all of this.

Just like with Netflix, you can stop the recording at any time, rewind it and listen to your "trouble" words and sounds as many times as you need to. Talk about learning at your own speed. All it takes to reduce your accent is a bit of effort and time invested.

There's at least one more item on the internet that could help you in reducing your Asian accent. That's called a podcast. In recent years, these internet audio files have exploded in popularity. Just like the YouTube videos you'll have no problem listening to what is essentially an internet radio program. You can anything from spiritual material to broadcasts on romance novels to . . . let your imagination start searching for your favorite topic. The next time your friends and family hear you speak English, they'll be astounded with your progress. And you'll be pretty pleased as well.

In the last two chapters you've learned not only why it's vital for you to reduce your Asian accent in this fast-paced global world, but you've just discovered on the best methods of doing this. Before you toss it aside or decide to search for another method to use, give some form of immersion a try. It'll work best when you attempt it on your terms.

In the next chapter, you'll be learning about how certain syllables in English are stressed or unstressed depending on any number of conditions. The stressing of specific syllables has been the downfall of many solid ESL students like yourself.

Once you overcome this, with the aid of the next chapter, you're taking a giant leap forward in sounding like a native speaker.

Chapter 3: First Things First: the Importance of Stressing Syllable

Of course, you feel frustrated at your difficulty in overcoming your accent. You're not alone, though. Consider this fact: there are nearly 1.6 million Chinese nationals now living in the United States. Of those, according to some accounts, nearly two-thirds of those individuals still speak with a distinguishable accent.

Imagine that! And that doesn't even take into account those who have come to the States from Japan and Korea in search of better jobs and education who retain their Asian accent.

Hopefully, knowing at least that much makes you feel a bit better about yourself. It does nothing, though, you're thinking, toward reducing the accent. You're right in that regard, of course, but that's what this chapter is for.

If you're at a loss at where to start, why not consider starting with the smallest portion of the English language – a single syllable. You're probably already aware that words are broken into syllables. For example, words composed only of a single syllable are box, fox, cat, bob, one, four . . .well, you get the idea.

According to linguists, the formal definition of a syllable as being the basic unit of a language containing only one vowel sound.

Words like doctor, socket, seven and trickster all possess two syllables. Most of the time, the average speaker isn't too concerned about this topic, unless of course you write poetry.

Syllables are responsible for the natural lyrical sounds many ascribe to the English language. Listen to a native speaker talk. If you listen close enough you can hear the "music" of his speech. Learning this rhythm can help you when you speak.

There are a few secrets to learning the rhythm. But don't expect any native speaker to tell you this because most Americans aren't aware of the secrets themselves.

In particular, if you follow five simple rules about stressing syllables you'll be that much closer to reducing your Asian accent. What do we mean "stressing" syllables? That's the syllable that you accent. When you listen to a native speaker, you'll understand just how this works.

But in addition to this, there are some rules governing how most English words are stressed in order to sound more like a natural-born speaker. Bear in mind, though, as you've probably already know far too well with the English language, that for every rule of pronunciation in the English language, there exist any number of exceptions.

These exceptions aren't in place intentionally to trip you up, regardless of what you believe in your moments of frustration. Instead, these exceptions are spread throughout the English language because it's borrowed such a variety of words freely from other languages worldwide.

Just when you're reeling from the number of exceptions, rest assured that of all the rules you're about to learn (or review) is the following one which – as of today – carries with it no exceptions.

In every English word containing more than one syllable, only one syllable is stressed.

Yes, it isn't a lot to go on, but look at it this way, it is something you can count on.

The other rules you're about to be provided can more often than not be followed, but not always. Be prepared to run across more than one exception.

1. **When a multi-syllable word contains a long vowel, the syllable containing that long vowel is stressed.**

Think of the word "colleague" or "suburbs."

2. **In nouns composed of two syllables, you'll be stressing the first syllable.**

Pronounce or get a native speaker to pronounce these sample words so you can become familiar with what this rule really means.

Apple
Pencil
Printer

The following words are examples of adjectives which also adhere to this rule.

Clever
Clumsy
Famous
Open

3. **If the words contain more than one syllable and are verbs, then the second syllable is accented.**

Consider – and pronounce – the words below:

To begin
To decide
To review

Of course, once again there are exceptions like:

To answer
To borrow

4. Place the stress on the next to the last syllable of the word when it ends in "ic," "sion," "tion," and "ious."

Pronounce the following words to get a feel for what it sounds like:

Allergic
Alcoholic
Eccentric
Geographic
Graphic

Adoption
Demonstration
Education
Exception
Information
Solution
Revelation

Conscious
Delicious

Glorious
Infectious

Here's a rule you'll love:

5. **For the words with the suffixes indicated below, the stress usually is on the syllable that is third from the last. The suffixes are: "cy," "al," "ate," "ise," or "ize" in the American spelling.**

Pronounce the following words so you can get familiar with how this rule sounds.

Democracy
Dependability
Geology
Photography
Sanity

Critical
Ethical
Geological

Supervise
Recognize
Advertise
Exercise

Now, that you've covered these, perhaps you recognize a pattern when you pronounce the following few family of words:

Equal
Equality
Equalize
Equalization

Final
Finality
Finalize
Finalization

Neutral
Neutrality
Neutralize
Neutralization

The stressing of syllables may be the perfect first step for you to take in your quest for reducing your Asian accent. Of course, this will, undoubtedly, take a bit of time. Don't let that distress you. Look how far you've come already in learning the English language.

Right now you're well on your way to perfecting all the hard work you've already given it.

The next area you'll begin to perfect is the pronunciation of the English consonants. These are unusually tough for Asian students, but by no means impossible. It all starts in the next chapter.

Chapter 4: The Trouble with Consonants . . . and Vowels

Yes, quite a few Asian students of English as a second language find that right after the proper stressing of syllables the correct way to enunciate consonants is their toughest area to master. There's a very good reason for this – and it has absolutely nothing with ability, your adaptability or even your desire to succeed.

This very often happens because the language commands that you make sounds that aren't in your native language and are completely new to you.

It's only natural, then, that the consonants will require a bit more work. Again, it's no reason to be discouraged. There's every reason to believe you can overcome this small bump in the road just like all the others you've encountered to so far.

Besides, once you realize what you need to do in order to conquer this problem, you'll know how small a problem it was to begin with. That's exactly what this chapter will help you do, realize how small a bump this entire consonant issue really is.

The same advice goes for the vowel sounds. Don't allow your current inability to pronounce them consume your thoughts and make you think you'll never be able to pronounce them. That's just all wrong. Thinking like that means you've defeated yourself even before you've started.

Let's start with, what is for most students, the most difficult consonants one to hear and distinguish. This ranks it right up there as one of the most difficult to correct. Let's face it, if you can't hear the difference, it's not easy to correct. With enough patience and consistency, though, you'll overcome it.

The Two "th" Sounds: Voiced and Unvoiced

The truth is that the voiced "th" and the unvoiced "th" are nearly identical. So what separates them? The way in which you move your tongue when you're pronouncing them. The voiced and unvoiced sounds not only share a common spelling, but they are nearly identical sounding, making it unusually hard to distinguish one sound from the other.

In each sound, however, the work of the tongue is the same. You'll place the tip of the tongue behind your front top teeth. In both sounds, a friction is created when these two areas meet. Not only that but don't be surprised if another, more subtle, type of friction appears between the tip of your tongue and the top front of your teeth as well.

During this entire period, hold your lips so that they are relaxed when you pronounce these sounds.

There is a second method of creating the "th" sound. This is to place the tip of your tongue in between your top teeth and your bottom front teeth. In this way, you'll still produce the proper sound. What it just may do, keep in mind, is to make it more difficult to transition to and from other sounds.

There's a simple enough reason for this, though. This is because the tongue is positioned farther forward than in the previous way.

Remember, too, that these sounds are referred to as "continuous consonants." This means that you should be able to hold them for a few seconds in an even and smooth pronunciation. Basically, you should encounter no trouble holding this sound for the entire length of the word.

The sounds are known as "fricatives," which give you an idea of how their pronunciation works. The majority of the fricative consonant sounds come from the friction of the air that's created when you speak the sound. It travels through a small opening in your vocal tract.

Both the voiced and unvoiced "th" sounds, as we have noticed share the same spelling. This means that the only way to really know which one to use is to memorize the pronunciation of new vocabulary words as you come across them.

As a general rule, the voiced "th" sound happens in far fewer words than the unvoiced ones. That being said, the voiced version is more common in what are called "function" words. These are parts of speech common used as pronouns, articles, and demonstratives.

Good examples of function words that are pronounced with a voiced "th" include the following list below.

The
That
Them
These
They
Their

Again, these are just a few of the words. Be prepared to meet more of them as you go along.

The Problematic Plural

Another problem for any Asians is pronouncing words in plurals in the English language. Plurals, as you well know, are forms of nouns that allows both the reader and your listener to recognize the number of that noun you're talking about. There is one cat and there are two cats.

Most English nouns can be easily turned into plurals with the simple addition of an "s" sound at the end of the word, as we saw in the previous paragraph. The complications arise depending on the type of consonant the "s" follows. Depending on that you'll discover that there are basically two sounds involved with this letter.

For the most part, when the "s" follows an unvoiced consonant, it keeps its original "s" sound. The words, cats, and kicks, are perfect examples of this. In each case, the reader knows immediately that the writer is talking about more than one of each.

However, if you were to create a plural for a word ending in an "r" sound, the letter "s" sounds more like a "z." Ask a native speaker to say the following words, so you can hear the subtle difference:

Computers
Sisters
Tears
Lowers
Others

Another instance in which the "s" at the end of a plural noun sounds like a "z" is when the word ends in the letter "w." Pronounce – or better yet, ask a native speaker to pronounce – the following prime examples of this rule:

Follows
Laws
News
Flaws
Throws
Thaws

Sometimes the "s" sound appears in the middle of words. When it's here, it also is doubled. As a general rule, you can be confident of pronouncing it properly – using the "s" and not the "z" sound. Think of hiss, miss, princess, bless and mess.

One final note on "s" sounds. This sound, for some reason, is difficult for many Asian students to pronounce when found at the start of a word. In many instances, Asians tend to pronounce it as a "sh" sound instead.

Most accent reduction experts believe that this problem can be considered a "structural" issue. That is, many students hold their teeth together too tightly when saying the "s" in this position of the word.

When pronouncing the following words, consciously relax your jaw:

See
Sudden
Strong
Special
Spin

That Stubborn "R" Sound

Perhaps the most difficult set of sounds for many Asian speakers are the "r" and the "l" sounds. These sounds seem to especially give Japanese students the most difficulty.

To many Asian students, these sounds may sound nearly identical. They are anything but that, though. There are several examples in English where placing the "l" for an "r" sounds transforms one word into a completely different word with a completely different meaning.

Take a look at the following three pairs of words and you'll immediately get the idea:

Glass
Grass

Law
Raw

Fry
Fly

To produce an "l" sound, the tip of your tongue must make contact with the top of your mouth – most specifically and ideally – your gums. Your tongue should end up right behind your top teeth.

By contrast, when you make the "r" sound your tongue doesn't touch any part of your mouth. Instead, your lips are pursed or slightly rounded. While your tongue should not be touching your mouth, you'll have difficulty if your tongue doesn't touch the sides of teeth, at least a bit.

By the time you've completed making this sound your tongue should be positioned in the middle of your mouth. Again, it should be touching any part of it though.

The "r" sound, in general, can also be difficult for Asians to pronounce when it comes at the end of a word. When placed here, linguists refer to this as the "r" vowel. Think of the words, car, sure, door floor and bar, just for starters.

This particular sound is made by keeping the back of your tongue flat. You'll also curve the tip of your tongue toward the upper teeth. At no time, though, should the tongue touch your teeth.

In addition to this, there should be a throaty sound when this sound is made. You'll know you're on the right track when you can feel the sound vibrate below your jaw.

When you overcome this pronunciation, many experts claim, you've created the perfect opportunity to get that much closer to your coveted American accent. This is especially true when the "r" ending is found in the stressed syllable of a multi-syllable. Pronounce (or have a native speaker) pronounce the following words:

Thirty

Terrible
Version
Verdict

The Importance of Vowels

If you're serious about reducing your accent, then it's vital that you master the vital vowel sounds. It's no wonder, as an Asian student, you feel as if you're having difficulty with your accent. In addition to these new sounds, you've got more than a few adjustments to make in your pronunciation of the vowels if you have any desire to reduce your accent.

Let's take a quick look at some of the most stubborn vowel sounds Asian ESL students encounter.

The Long "A"

The most common error Asian students make with this sound is pronouncing it as a short "e." To say this sound properly the long "a" needs to start off and end up with what's known as a "tense vowel."

Keep in mind that in your quest to reduce your accent, this small seemingly simple sound establishes you as a native speaker. Most Asian students will relax the sound, making the word the word "date" sound like the word "debt."

Here are a few other words you can pronounce, remembering while you pronounce these that you should keep this sound tense:

Take
Space
Became
Playing
Aim
Await

The Long "U"

Many times, the Asian student reaches for a nasal sound when he says a long "u." It is, however, a much fuller and richer sound than that. It almost resonates in the chest. When the Asian student says the word "rude," for example, the American ear often hears the word "rid."

When pronouncing this sound, you want to be sure that the pitch of the sound descends a bit. This is especially vital when it appears in stressed syllables. Think of the words super, future, stupid and summon.

If you can't detect the sound yourself, ask a friend to pronounce these words as well. He'll be able to help you hear them.

The Long "I"

The only real difficulty Asian students may find with the long "i" sound is in pronouncing it clearly enough. The most common mispronunciation is to add an almost unnoticeable "uh" sound right before actually enunciating the vowel. When said in this fashion, it sounds almost like a short "u" sound.

It's nearly undetectable when you say this vowel, but if you listen closely, the sound begins with the short "o" sound.

A good hint is to keep the long "i" sounding sharp and bright. Pronounce the following words to get a feel for the sound:

High

Fly
Life
Diary
Believe

If it seems like the English language has a lot going on with its pronunciation, it's because, honestly, it does. And if you sat down and tried to memorize all these rules, you may never open your mouth again in public and try to pronounce anything. If you're stressing the right syllable, you think, you probably are missing the proper and correct enunciation of one of the vowels . . . or maybe the consonants. . oh heck maybe you're pronouncing everything wrong.

Don't worry! Every person who has ever learned a new language has felt this way at one time or another. The point is that you get over it and you start using a few techniques in which the rules aren't as important as listening to native speakers themselves.

Move on to the next chapter to learn about a few effective techniques that not only will have you listening to native speakers, but have you speaking like one in no time at all.

Chapter 5: Choose a Method, Any Method of Accent Reduction

You've become quite knowledgeable during the journey of this book not only about the sounds that trip most Asian students when they start seriously attempting to reduce their accent. But you're learning some effective ways at which to go about doing it.

In a very real sense, we've covered many topics that can clearly be labeled academic. Now's let's spend a bit of time learning some of the more "hands-on," practical methods of reducing your accent.

To be honest, there are quite a few excellent techniques and methods you can easily implement, short of immersing yourself completely in the English language, as we mentioned earlier in this book.

The Reverse Accent Mimicry Technique

It sounds incredible and quite unlikely that it would even work, but every person who's tried it says it does.

Not only does it work, but for some the reduction in accent is and potentially permanent.

Willing to give it a try if you can even get a fraction of these results?

Reverse Accent Mimicry is almost too good to be true, but more and more students are discovering it every day and giving it rave reviews. The premise is quite simple. You start with finding a native English speaker with a thick accent when speaking your native language.

Listen closely to the pronunciation and the cadence of his speech. As a native speaker of the language he's learning, you'll immediately recognize his problem areas.

Guess what? The difficulties he has when speaking your language can view in a very real sense as the problems you're encountering when speaking English

Here's how reverse accent mimicry works. The premise for this technique is that you speak your native language following this person as closely as possible – poor accent and all the other blemishes. In the long run, it's those poor pronunciations and other blemishes that are going to help you.

You'll notice as you do this the structural and grammar problems the individual encounters with your language. If you take this exercise seriously, you'll be amazed at how quickly you'll lose your accent.

The "Listen and Repeat" Method

The following method is fairly easy. It involves listening to a native speaker present a recorded presentation. With the internet and youtube, this is really much easier than it ever has been.

You'll want to listen to about fifteen seconds or so of the presentation at a time before stopping the recording. Now, repeat everything the speaker said, again paying special attention as in the previous technique to the rhythm of his words as well as his pronunciation.

Don't be too concerned about what the topic is. In fact, you're encouraged to choose one you have a personal or professional interest in. When you do this, you're much more likely to sit and listen – and absorb – for a greater period of time.

The purpose, as you probably already guessed, is to become more familiar with the various sounds of the English language and in the process mimic them.

The two techniques presented so far are based on actually speaking the language and aren't that concerned with the so-called rules of pronunciation.

Sometimes, when you focus excessively on the rules, you trip up, slow yourself down – or even talk yourself out of your goal.

There are certain instructors who prefer their student to practice this technique instead of watching television with an ear to accent reduction. The reason?

Those individuals who give form presentations usually speak more clearly. You may want to give this a try and see for yourself.

Listen to Yourself

That's right! This method, which seems obvious, is a perfect opportunity to hear yourself as others hear you speak English. Perhaps the hardest part for most students is the necessity of listening to your own voice. Most people don't realize the true timber of their own voice and seldom give it much thought. So coming "ear to ear" with it, as it were is sometimes a rude awakening. Brace yourself for it.

Once you get past this, you'll then be able to focus on your pronunciation of the English language. This exercise will bring you face to face with the true extent of your accent.

Many students perform this exercise at the start of their program and periodically after that check in to determine the extent of their progress. It's actually an extremely rewarding way to see that you truly are making progress – even during those low points when you feel as if you're not.

Shadowing As a Method of Accent Reduction

Shadowing is an ingenious if simple, method of reducing your accent. And it really doesn't have a thing to do with following someone around town in their shadow, regardless of what it sounds like.

Simply stated, it involves you listening to an audio production. As with the other methods, this exercise works best when you choose a topic in which you have some degree of interest.

Your goal is to listen and then repeat what's being said as quickly as possible after it has been spoken. This allows you to experience the best effects of this technique. Your goal in actuality is to repeat the words at the same time that they are being said.

Now, that you understand the basis and basics of shadowing, you may want to raise this practice to another level. You may want to try physically walking while you're shadowing your recorded presentation. You'd be surprised by adding a small physical action such as this can be such a springboard to reducing your accent.

The point of this effective technique is to make you sound as close to a native speaker as quickly as possible.

The several suggestions presented in this chapter are void – as I'm sure you've already noticed – of any of the rules, laws, do's and don'ts of English grammar. While all those rules are important, you can learn the language without parroting back all the rules of grammar and pronunciation.

Think about it for a moment. That's actually how most native speakers learned. At the knees of their parents, without any interest at all in the laws. Learning the rules will follow in their due time.

In the conclusion, we talk briefly about the need to outline a strategy before you jump blindly into these techniques. After all, if you set off with some plan, then you'll have an effective and efficient way of measuring your success. And you're virtually guaranteed to succeed.

Conclusion

Overwhelmed? Frustrated?

Were those your feelings when you choose to read this book? Perhaps you felt you were asking too much of yourself when you set off to reduce or even eliminate your Asian accent when speaking English.

That's a natural enough feeling. Your goal then, at the least, was the hope of finding a gem of a suggestion or a revelation of a secret to kick-start the development of a true accent-free speech. With any luck, you found an abundance of methods to help you not only raise your consciousness of your flaws when speaking the English language but techniques to overcome them.

The one essential ingredient required in order to speak like a native, though, is something that's difficult to teach. That's because the desire to overcome your accent comes from you – all the external motivation in the world isn't going to improve your accent one iota if you don't have the will to do it.

In a nutshell, it's called self-discipline. You can have all the desire that's humanly possible, but if you don't work on improving your speech every day, you'll make some progress, of course. But the improvement will not occur nearly as fast as if you practice some consistency and persistency in speaking the language.

In this scenario, also, it's very possible to lose our zest for perfecting the language – and that would be a shame. After all, you've worked so hard to get this far. Think back to the self-discipline you had just to get to the point where you are today.

Yes, this is exactly where self-discipline comes into play. Nobody can burn the self-discipline into you. There are, however, action steps you can take – both in the overall scheme of reducing your accent and in the specific smaller chunks and steps you take daily (Yes, why, of course daily!) to consciously work toward your goal.

7 Successful Steps to Accent Reduction for Asian Students

Follow the seven steps outlined below and you're virtually guaranteed to hear an amazing improvement in how close you come to speaking like a native. You'll discover in a matter of months, perhaps even weeks, you'll sound more like a native speaker than ever before.

1. **Set a start date when you plan to pledge all the resources you have at hand to overcoming your Asian accent.**

You're tempted, I'm sure, to jump right in and to fix everything at once. That may be a serendipitous result of the immersion record. And indeed, eventually, that may be exactly the technique you'll choose.

But before you do that, give yourself a breather – at least a couple of days to collect your wits and prepare yourself mentally for your journey of self-discipline.

By preparing yourself mentally in this way, many psychologists tell us, that you'll get vastly improved – and quicker – results than just jumping in without thinking a plan through. Choosing a date also marks that moment as a commitment and not just a whimsical "someday in the future" notion.

2. Develop a strategy

You have the date. Your next decision is in the development of a strategy. Don't worry! It's not as difficult as it sounds. If you're lie most students you have several difficult areas in your speech you can't wait to tackle. That's good. You've got enthusiasm. But before you go just trying a bit of this and a bit of that. Step back (Here's another reason to set a date! To develop a sure-fire strategy.) to reflect on what is the most effective way to reduce your accent.

Decide how you're going to tackle your problem areas. Of course, your strategy may indeed, involve the immersion method in which you do attempt to correct all of your flaws at once. After all, you've jumped in speaking nothing but English, that's what you'd expect to occur.

It could be though you're not that adventurous. And that's okay too. But then you'll want to develop a plan if you opt to correct one area at a time. In that case, you've got some decisions to make:

What area will be the first you tackle? Will you opt to correct what you perceive as your worst, knowing that the rest couldn't be nearly as difficult?

Then, you may want to repair what you perceive as the easiest – or just let's say the least difficult – of them, in order to provide yourself with a quick sense of satisfaction and accomplishment. In this way, you've not only boosted your ability to speak like a native, but also your self-confidence. That's always a good thing.

Once you've decided a specific area, then you may want to place a time limit on practicing that one area until you go on to the next. The hope is that you've overcome that particular trouble spot, but if you haven't, you can always approach it again. If you stick with one area to look, you're sure to become bored with it.

3. Choose a technique or techniques

This volume has provided you with several techniques as well variations of techniques to help you overcome your accent. Now is the time to decide – at least initially – which you think will work best for you considering the strategy you choose and your personal learning style.

Here's another piece of advice that many students don't realize. Once you choose a technique, you don't have to stay with it. Especially if you don't hear any progress. If you thought the immersion process would work on one area and you haven't reduced your accent, then move on to another technique.

Nor do you need to use the same technique for each flaw you have that prevents you from speaking like a native. If immersion helped with your voicing your consonants better, that doesn't mean it's going to be a technique that will help you with your vowel sounds. And you may decide you want a completely different technique when it comes to learning how to stress the syllables in your word.

You can outline now what technique you plan to use on which flaw. Or if you don't have a clue how you'll respond to a particular method, start with something that seems to make sense and continue trying new techniques until you find something that works for you.

4. Set priorities.

This is of utter importance and can't be said too often: set priorities.

You'd be surprised how many ways in which you can do this. What areas are you going to give more attention to? Are you going to treat each of these flaws equally? Or do you plan on giving several extra days for some of the most difficult areas?

These are some decisions you'll be able to make right now. Some of these priorities you may need to adjust as you discover your ability to overcome them. There very well could be a trouble spot that you thought would be much more difficult to overcome than it was. You may not use the entire two weeks you allotted for its practice. In that case, adjust your schedule and move on to your next area. For the moment, at least, you'll find yourself ahead of schedule. Isn't that a boost in your self-confidence?

Similarly, you may discover that an area you thought you could conquer more quickly is becoming something of a sticking point with you. Don't be afraid to be flexible and adjust your priorities – even it means extending your completion date. As long as you're working on reducing your accent, you're following your overall plan.

6. Inform a few close friends and some trusted family members.

You'll want to tell a few people whom you trust exactly what you're doing. These are the individuals you're going to ask to hold you accountable in accomplishing these seven steps. It's vital, then, that you trust them completely.

This means right from the start, you know they'll be in your corner, cheering for you. When you doubt your ability or staying power, these are the persons who'll tell you that, indeed, you can do it.

These are also the people who will be the first to know when you've reached or exceeded your goals. These are the friends who will sincerely rejoice with you when you've overcome your accent.

Choose them wisely.

7. Select a definite ending date.

This ending date, depending on the progress you've made, may not be the actual final date of practice. If you haven't mastered the language by that time, don't worry. What do you do in that case? You simply assess your progress to see what you need to work on next.

It would be wise to wait at least a few days to a week, then to regroup yourself and see what's left. Then you'll start these seven steps again. If you have to perform these steps again, as many students do, never think of it as a failure. Consider it another massive move forward in your ability to speak English like a native.

Because that's exactly what it is.

Bonus:

Public Speaking Secrets

How To Deliver A Perfect Presentation as a Foreign
Professional

Whitney Nelson

Chapter 1: Stage Fright Speaks in Every Language, but . . .

Milosh sat at the coffee shop staring at his cappuccino when his friend Raj saw him. Asking if he could sit with him, Raj commented that it looked as if he were deep in thought.

Milosh readily opened up. "English isn't your first language, Raj. You've spoken in public. Weren't you the least bit nervous?"

"But, of course, I was" he said quickly. "Are you scheduled to speak?"

"Yeah, and this is important. If I do a good job, I may be on the shortlist for the promotion at work. No pressure here, right?" He paused, took a sip of coffee and looked his friend in the eye, as if asking for advice. Finally, he asked, "How do I survive this, let alone speak coherently enough to win that promotion?"

Have you found yourself in Milosh's position? Do you have nightmares about being in such a position? If you believe it's impossible to present a coherent, well-received public presentation while speaking your second language, English, think again.

You shouldn't be surprised if you experience stage fright when you're invited to speak before an audience – or even to give a presentation to a small group of individuals at work.

Even individuals who have spoken English all their lives know what stage fright feels like. Of course, I understand this innate fear may very well be heightened when English is your second language. I agree, it feels as if that one element throws an entirely new perspective on the event.

But that doesn't mean you can't conquer it. There are some easy ways to overcome stage fright – even when you're speaking in your second language.

In this chapter we investigate the reasons why you – speaking in your second language – may feel the bite of stage fright a bit more than native speakers. We'll even offer you methods that have worked for so many that reduce that fear as much as possible.

Broadly speaking, the fears are formed around five broad concerns.

Fear # 1 – I'm embarrassed by my foreign accent

Many individuals who speak English as a second language have that very same fear: What about my foreign accent? This fear not only includes a general embarrassment of your so-called accent, but the potentially devastating effects you mistakenly believe it may have on your presentation.

Let's get one thing straight right now, even the most polished speakers are sometimes misunderstood. I'm not only talking about those who speak English as a second language, but native American speakers can easily be misunderstood in their own language.

Right now, I'm sure you're not real concerned about those whose first language is English. But what if I told you that even one of the most famous non-native English speakers have been misunderstood when giving a presentation.

Even the Dalai Lama can be Misunderstood

Who? The Dalai Lama. Yes, the Tibetan leader was speaking at Brown University. The closed-caption transcriptionist mistook his saying the word "forget" for another, albeit, rather offense swear word, also beginning with the letter "f."

The context in which this happened appeared simple enough, at least on the surface. The great spiritual leader said that if his listeners had found his ideas thought-provoking, to please share them with others. If not, then they could simply "forget." That's not what the transcriptionist heard or typed.

It's unlikely that such a mistake will happen to you. And should it does happen, you can at least take some solace in knowing it's also happened to none other than the Dalai Lama. So now that we've tried to assuage your fears some, let's emphasize that accents shouldn't be embarrassing.

Many individuals will actually spend more time listening to you speak (as long as they can understand you) with your accent than without. There are always those persons who are enthralled listening to the intonation as well as the meaning of the words.

According to some, that wasn't the first time audience members have mistaken his word "forget" for the other, less tolerated (and much less spiritual) word. Have you heard that he has given up talking in English in public? Absolutely not.

So, let's just push that fear right out of your mind. Not that I'm discouraging you from taking measures to reduce your accent. If you feel that would make you a better public speaker, then the moment you know you need to make a public presentation, then by all means start practicing exercises that will help overcome your accent.

Fear #2: What if I can't find the right English words for my topic.

This can be a fear you can simply drop in the trash. You'll have absolutely no problems searching for the correct word as long as you keep on practicing your presentation.

This piece of news is nothing new, speakers have known about it for years. The more you've prepared your speech – in essence work with words – the easier the proper words will pop into your mind.

This doesn't' matter if your first language is Spanish or Italian. Practice the words that surround your area of interest. The more words you can use when you talk, the better your speech will be. While you're searching for one word using a thesaurus or other word will eventually be followed by even more words.

If you know your topic, chances are you won't forget words. Of course, if you do forget an occasional word, it's not the end of the world. Here, again, even native speakers forget words. Recover and move on. Just keep in mind while you're practicing for this event, that the better acquainted you are with your topic, the least likely you are to forget a word.

Many speakers – regardless of their first language – may forget a word or two simply because they're under stress. That's why practicing can help. It will lessen the stress on you, making it far less likely for you to forget a word here or there or even chunks of your presentation.

You can easily understand why adequate preparation can help relieve your stress and in turn make it easier for your mind to recall the words you need whether it's in your native language or not.

There are still two more tricks you can easily put into effect to help practically ensure that you don't forget a word or two. The first is through preparing the "vocabulary" that forms the majority of your presentation and rehearse it continuously. If you know that every topic has "most used" words and phrases, you'll be wise to study them and, specifically, say them out loud as often as you can.

The second trick is to place special emphasis and concentration on the start of your presentation. By this, I don't mean to emphasize the beginning of your speech to the exclusion of the rest of it. The very first few minutes of this speech are critically important to your success. When you start off on the right foot, as they say, the better and easier it'll be for you to develop the rest of your topic.

By emphasizing the beginning of your presentation and nailing it, you'll also increase your self-confidence dramatically.

Fear # 3 – Is my English going to be easily Understood?

It's a natural fear that you believe that some individuals in the audience may not understand your English. If you speak with an accent, you're probably repeating yourself because people didn't quite grasp what you said the first time around.

But, once again (and I'm sure you're getting tired of me saying it) even some native speakers are tough to understand when they get to the podium to speak.

Your audience will find it much easier understanding you, when you structure your presentation properly, that is, in a logical progress. This ensures that those listening to the speech will be able to follow the flow of your presentation with ease. When it flows, your audience doesn't need to fumble around spending time thinking about how to piece your information together. That gives them more time to listen and comprehend you.

We'll talk more about structure in a later chapter. The way in which you structure your presentation depends on its goal. You'll prepare and structure your talk differently for different messages. This will help your audience in understanding you.

Secondly, much of what we call communication is simply the use of intonation of the language. Your audience is not only listening to what words you say, but also how you say them. A sure way to get their attention – and keep it – is to sound expressive as well as friendly.

Sounding "expressive" really shouldn't be much of a problem. If you're giving a presentation, it's probably about a topic you're at least interested in, if not passionate about. If you can convey your enthusiasm for the topic, then that will filter through to your audience and they'll be enthusiastic too.

More than that, though, your intonation also reflects how your audience perceives the meaning of your words. The identical sentence, spoken with different emphases on different words, can and does take on different meanings.

Here's a quick example of what I mean. Think of the sentence: "I'm sure he'll think of a better plan."

When no one word is stressed above any other it's just a general statement. It carries no implications or connotations. Now, say that same sentence only emphasize the word "better." This hints that that first plan was less than good.

If you say it emphasizing "he'll" in the sentence, then that implies he is critical of the first plan and may not have even been the creator of it.

When the word "sure" is stressed then you're expressing the fact that there is no doubt in your mind that he can think of a better plan.

As you can see, there are plenty of ways to interpret this sentence depending on the emphasis of your words. Every sentence you speak – especially in your presentation – can be taken and interpreted in a variety of ways, depending on your intonation.

Fear # 4 – I'm afraid my presentation will be boring because I speak too slowly

If this is your fear, you'll be surprised to learn it's really your strength. That's right!

You're aware that it's natural for you to speak in your second language more slowly than you speak in your native tongue. But up to this point you may have considered it a weakness. At this very moment, it has now become a strength. Congratulations!

This is one area of using your developing language you don't have to worry about. Native speakers are constantly told to slow down when speaking in public. If there is one major criticism – especially those who aren't used to standing in front of the podium -- it's they speak too fast. Their natural rapidity of speech is then exaggerated due to the stress they feel while they are speaking.

I have a friend whose first language is English. He'll practice his presentation, even timing it, ensuring it's just the right length. He doesn't go over his allotted time and he's provided time for questions and answers.

Do you know what happens when he actually gets in front of the audience? He shaves even more time off the presentation because he talks faster than he's ever done in his practice sessions. He speaks even faster because he's nervous.

When you're speaking in public, you can't use the same flow of words as in a normal, casual conversation. Why? Because your presentation (hopefully) contains new information for the audience to digest. They need the time. If they're still trying to process that last sentence you said while you've already covered three more sentences, you've lost them.

That's not fair to them – they aren't receiving all the information you want them to have – or to you. They're missing out on something important you want to convey and have been practicing. Speak too fast and it's a lose-lose situation for everyone.

The best speakers adjust the pace of their speech. By doing this, they ensue that their listeners totally understand what's being said.

The use of the subtle pauses in your speech also conveys certain meanings and adds emphasis to what you're saying. It works, in fact, very much like intonation does. Let's look at the words in this sentence, "If all of us do our share, we will succeed!"

Read it out loud. It could have any number of meanings when read with little enthusiasm and too quickly. Now see how the entire meaning of the sentence changes when you place pauses in all the right places. "If (pause) all of us (pause) do our share (pause) we will succeed!"

Can you see how the second sentence is stronger than the first?

Fear # 5 – Will I understand the audience's questions?

The question-and-answer portion of a speech generates the most fear for most individuals who speak English as a second language. Why? Because they feel as if they aren't in control. They feel they can't rehearse or prepare for potential questions.

Rest assured, that there are even professional speakers who present in their first language who are also intimidated by this portion of the presentation. Opening the floor up to questions is quite risky. You never know who's about to ask what kind of question.

There really are methods you can use to provide you with the self-confidence you need to get you through this portion of the event.

First, you need to convince your inner fear-monger that you really aren't walking into a lion's den unprepared. That's really the truth. You've undoubtedly prepared quite a while on this presentation. All you need to do is to spend just a little bit more time and anticipate – based on what you're talking about – the potential audience questions.

Take a good, long look at your topic. What parts of the speech are most likely to produce the most questions? This becomes fairly easy if you're presenting any controversial or new ideas. Right away, you can count on someone challenging them or at the very least desiring to learn more about them.

Once you have identified these parts, then you can just about guess off the top of your head what questions you'll be asked. Secondly, keep in mind that you are the expert. Look at you. You're the individual standing at the podium. You're the person talking to the audience. That point should not be lost on you. Trust me, it's not lost on the audience. It means (in case you need reminding) that you know your material very well.

Simply put, if you've prepared every other part of your speech, then you'll be able to handle the question-and-answer session – even if English is your second language.

If your fear, as a speaker of English as a second language, is that you won't understand a question, here are a few strategies you can employ to buy you a bit more time before you answer.

Simply ask the audience member to repeat the question under the pretense that you didn't hear it.

Ask the questioner to clarify what he means. In this way, you'll have another chance to hear the question (from a different angle, perhaps) while you're planning your response.

This brings us to the final question in this part. What if, despite everything, you really don't know the answer to one of the questions? Don't panic. It happens to everyone. Simply admit you don't know the answer, that you've never been confronted with the question before this, but that you certainly would be happy to investigate it further. After all, you may decide to add, you're eager to know the answer as well.

In this chapter, we've talked about preparation as the key to gaining any confidence in public speaking. In the following chapter we'll provide you with a few of the keys to prepare yourself for your big day.

Chapter 2: Practice your English Before you're scheduled to Present

MIlosh sat at his favorite coffee shop reading his notes. His public speaking engagement was fast approaching and he wanted to be doubly sure that he was prepared.

Some of his friends chided him for taking the event so seriously. "Just relax and be yourself," they told him. "There is something called over-preparedness. You already know the material backward and forward, inside and out. What more can you do?"

Milosh, the wise man that he is, ignored this advice. No one needed to tell him he was an expert in his area. That aspect of his public speaking engagement gave him little concern. The part that kept him up at night, figuratively speaking, was the actual speaking.

You've probably have heard this particular advice over and over again. I'm betting you've been told this so much that its full implications may not even register with you much anymore.

It comes to you in two words: be confident. Not only will your friends and family tell you this, but go to any website on public speaking and they'll tell you the same thing. Self-confidence is the key to a speech well presented.

Unfortunately, few of these well-intended people and sites actually tell you how you gain this self-confidence. Sure some of them start out by saying, "act as if" you already have it and it will eventually settle on your shoulder like a butterfly.

Excuse me, since I've never had a butterfly settle on my shoulder, I'm not sure I'm going to depend on this method. Sure, I can act as if, but I sure hope I have something else in my pocket to bolster my confidence.

What many people don't tell you is that you need to be thoroughly prepared in order to gain that elusive self-confidence.

It's true. The more you prepare, the more self-confidence you'll gain. So instead of lecturing you on the fact that you should have self-confidence, like it's a commodity you can go to the corner store and buy off the shelf, I'm going to provide you with a few tips on how you can thoroughly prepare for your public speaking engagement. If you follow and practice these even occasionally, you'll find your self-confidence about talking in your second language grow.

No Time Like the Present.

This is a politely subtle way of saying "this is not a time to procrastinate."

Indeed, it isn't. When should you start preparing for your engagement? If your answer is the moment you're assigned or invited, then you get a gold star. You're absolutely right.

Waiting till the last minute to prepare a speech may work for some people. But it seldom works for those who are presenting in a second language. Allow yourself as much time as possible to prepare.

In fact, it isn't that outrageous of an idea to give yourself an extra week – even two – if you can to focus on this presentation.

Don't Trust Your Memory to Speak Off the Cuff

You may have notice that some individuals have the talent of speaking extemporaneously. Just jumping off on the spur of the notice and presenting a perfectly structured, finely delivered speech. Or so it may seem so to the audience.

It's true. Some individuals can do this, but more often than not, somewhere along the line, these people have been planning this moment. Sure, they probably weren't scheduled, but in their minds they've probably rehearsed what they would say if they ever got the chance to speak.

Not only that, but they've probably been practicing their English skills as well, in hopes of one day being able to speak in this manner. What appears to be unplanned and off the cuff was probably months in the making.

Write the Speech Out in English.

No, you won't read your speech from your notes, but there are so many advantages to writing it out. First and foremost, the simple act of writing it out will clarify your thoughts.

If you opt to write it in your native language and translate it, you may find that, upon translation, may lead to improper sentence structure as well as some poor phrasing.

Read Your Speech Out Loud

Once you've written your speech, then it's time to read it out loud. This will help you feel more comfortable with the pronunciation of words that may give you a difficult time. This also is valuable in listening to the proper sentence structure of these ideas in English.

And by the way, read it more than once. Reading it more than once provides you with the familiarity you'll need in order to give a first-class, professional style. But more than that, this form of preparedness will give you the confidence you probably never knew you had.

Create a Set of Notes based on your Speech.

Yes. You read that correctly. Once you've written the speech out and read it a few times, then you'll want to take notes on it. These don't have to be extensive notes. They can be fairly simple – enough even to give you a hint of where you're going next in the presentation. If you even create an outline, you'll find this to be of great help. These notes should not be written out in full sentences as much as you think that method would be better.

Instead, the purpose of these notes is to help you keep track of where you are in your presentation as well as where you're headed. If you write out full sentences instead, you may discover this method awkward when you consult them.

Practice Presenting your Speech

Did you really think I would neglect to tell you this? This is one of the most important steps to preparedness. In fact, the ultimate practice session is to give this presentation to a native-speaking friend or two.

This may go without saying, but I'll say it anyway, the more often you can give these practice presentations, the better your presentation will be. In turn, you'll find yourself gaining self-confidence not only in your trial runs, but when you eventually stand in front of that audience.

There is a key to this suggestion, though. Many individuals read their speech in front of friends and family who tell them how great it is. Before your trial run, explain to your "beta listeners" that you want feedback – honest feedback.

Of course, we all want positive feedback, but not at the expense of the quality of our speech. Explain to your listeners that you want – indeed – need their honest criticism. Promise them you won't take it personally. Then, don't take it personally. Instead, think about the reason for constructive criticism for what it's meant to be– a means to make you a better speaker in English.

Record your Presentation during your Practice Sessions

This is critical in truly learning how you sound when you speak in public. Your first thought upon hearing this is to simply record your voice. Give consideration, though, to actually video-taping yourself as well. When you do this, you may find your body language is less than inviting. Or it could be that your body language or posture doesn't match with what you're saying.

You'll also discover when you do this, you may become your worse critic. Take your own criticism with a grain of salt. Sure, you may never get to the level of perfection that you desire, but that doesn't mean you should give up. It may just mean, for one thing, that you're expecting a bit too much from yourself at the moment.

Remember, too, that you've started earlier in preparing than most people just because you know it's going to take you a bit longer to get yourself to the point where you're satisfied.

Reverse Accent Mimicry

Many speakers who present in their second language tend to worry about their accent. English has a few sounds which no other language has – perhaps some of these sounds are new to you. On top of that, though, when you speak English you may become confused by the stress or emphasis of syllables within the words. This is exactly where reverse accent mimicry can help you overcome these hurdles that so many ESL students seem to stumble over.

It could be that right now, knowing you have a speaking engagement in your future, you're concerned about how your listeners will accept and understand your accent.

The concept behind this practice is easy enough. The method simply involves analyzing an English speaker who has a strong English accent speaking in your language. If Spanish is your first language, for example, then you're o searching for someone who speaks Spanish with a thick American accent.

What you're going to do is to speak your native language, in this case, Spanish, as your model is speaking it. Be sure to imitate everything – and I mean everything – the person is saying and how he is saying it. Incorporate all his "mistakes" from difficulties in pronunciation to the grammar issues and the structural difficulties.

The problems that this person has when speaking your language, can reversibly reflect the problems that you will have when speaking English.

When you do this, you'll discover, much to your surprise, that this is a quantum leap in perfecting your own English pronunciation and reducing your accent.

Practice. Record, repeat. Review.

Ask any language instructor. The best way to become fluent in a language is to use it – as often as possible. So it should come as no surprise to learn that by reading your presentation out loud, recording it, then listening to is one of the quickest and easiest ways to become proficient at delivering your speech.

Not only that, but the instructions for doing so, are as simple reading the instructions on a bottle of shampoo: lather, rinse, repeat. In this case, practice, record, repeat, and review. You've no doubt taken more than enough courses in the English language that these instructions are a well-worn mantra. But just because it isn't a creative approach to practicing for your big day, doesn't mean it's not an effective one. Because it certainly is. In fact, it's one of the most effective, despite its mundane and tedious application.

When you're using this method for your presentation, you simply record yourself reading or better yet, presenting it from your outline without notes – and then listen to the recording. While you should be critical, don't be overly so. Choose one or two areas you'd like to improve in initially and study these diligently. See how many items you can improve upon in the time you have.

Do this until your comfortable presenting your speech, not only the material itself and the outline, but also the intonation of your voice and the stress you place on the syllables of your words and the pauses among your words themselves.

Alternate your Practice Material

But you can take this form of rehearsal one step further. Because inevitably your presentation will become routine for you, alternate reading and repeating your speech with reading other materials. You may want to read a novel, using all the forms of emotion the author intended for the characters to possess.

Do everything you did with your speech, but just practice it with the book. This will keep you speaking English and not boring yourself or sliding into bad habits because you've read your material too many times. Choose a book you've been longing to read and this should keep your interest for a while. In fact, if you choose your reading material wisely, it won't seem the least bit tedious, it may even become a pleasure.

Of course, your selection of exactly what to read out loud and how you do this are only limited by your own imagination. Below are some materials as well as ways to institute this practice if reading novels get boring.

Are you a news hound or a political junkie? Then why not try reading a newspaper or even a web site devoted to news or politics. Select a story in a printed newspaper or magazine or one on a web site. Read it out loud recording yourself as you go along. Play the recording back, listening to yourself critically. Then record yourself again, searching for ways to improve your speaking.

Do this at least once a day once you've been assigned or committed yourself to the public speaking engagement. This is a form of rehearsal you can easily start even before you've written your speech simply by reading books, magazines, newspapers as well as web sites out loud.

Once you begin composing your speech, you then can record snippets of the speech, listen to yourself – and to the actual writing – and know how you sound and, as an added bonus, how well your speech is written.

If you've given yourself the two-week practice time as we've suggested earlier, you'll have plenty of time to correct any words that may be tripping you up. So, there's no need to get frustrated or worried.

Listen to Four Areas

As you listen with an ear to improve your speaking voice, there are four areas in particular that are critical. They're listed below:

Pronunciation and Enunciation

You may think that this goes without saying, but when you speak in public it's doubly important. For one thing, your first goal is to make it as easy as possible for your audience to understand – and not question – what you've just told them. This means that when you express yourself you place the emphasis on the proper syllable or syllables in the words. I've said it before and I'll say it again. You don't want your audience questioning what you said and entirely missing a chunk of vital information that follows.

Make sure you're not mumbling and that each and every word is pronounced clearly. When you are doing this correctly, you may feel as if your mouth is working overtime, exaggerating the movements of your jaw and lips. Don't worry about that. Record yourself. If your words sound clear when your listen to them, then you can rest assured your mouth isn't in any exaggerated position.

Projection

I know. I know. You're going to have a microphone to amplify your voice. You really don't need to worry about that. But you do – even with a microphone. When you learn how to project your voice, speaking from your diaphragm, then not only will you sound naturally louder but more authoritative as well.

This means, should any mishap occur with the electronics you will still be able to carry on. Not only that, when you speak louder, people automatically assume you're more knowledgeable about a subject. Any doubts you may have in your own mind about them not taking you as seriously as you wish because of the way you speak English will vanish. And that's always a good thing!

Your use of inflection

You might not be able to provide a good definition off the top of your head of the word inflection, but you know it when you hear it. Let's just say you immediately recognize it when you don't hear inflection.

You've probably sat through enough college lectures in which the professors couldn't or felt they didn't need to utilize this tool. The result? Boring courses in which very few students learned much if anything at all! You were subjected to monotone speakers who had more than one student sleeping and many struggling to stay awake. That's not exactly the reaction you want from your audience, now is it?

Instead, you want to make your presentation as entertaining and engaging as possible. And before you say that it's impossible with your topic, think about the TED talks that have become increasingly popular thanks to YouTube and NPR or National Public Radio.

What does TED stand for? Technology, Entertainment and Design. Notice that the "E" stands for entertainment – not education. While it's a given your presentation will educate your audience, consider that in order to maintain their attention, it should also entertain. Part of the way in which to do this is through a vivid presentation. And that definitely involves the inflection of your voice.

Listening to your Cadence

You've no doubt heard the word cadence before as well. Sometimes it's used when individuals talk about the pace of soldiers walking together. While we're talking words, the meaning is similar. When I mention cadence, I'm referring to the pace of your delivery. Just like you can bore your audience without using varying degrees of inflection, you can do the same with your cadence – or lack thereof.

Listen to your presentation paying strict attention to the speed of your delivery. Is every sentence spoken at the same pace? Is it excruciating slow or do you quicken the pace every now and then based on the emotion you're conveying and on the content of your presentation?

When you can slow what you say at critical points you want to emphasize and want the audience to truly comprehend, you can feel comfortable they've received the message. By the same token, if you're telling a story involved in your topic, you might want to speed your pace or cadence to indicate a higher degree of excitement. Again, this is where the TED talks are one of the best examples around of this.

Pauses

A well-defined pause is as important in a talk as the use of any other form of communication. Pauses, when positioned correctly, can build tension if you like (watch any television reality show to confirm this) and to allow your audience to really concentrate on what you've just said.

They're also critical if you've added humor into your speech. A well-timed pause will give your listeners the time to laugh without worrying that they're missing something you've just said.